How to Declutter with Archangel Jophiel

How to relieve stress, anxiety, and clutter from your life

Copyright © 2018 Z.Z. Rae

All rights reserved. This book contains material protected under International and Federal Copyright Laws and Treaties. Any unauthorized reprint or use of this material is prohibited. No part of this book may be reproduced or transmitted in any form or by any means, electronic or mechanical, including photocopying, recording, or by any information storage and retrieval system without express written permission from the author/publisher

Café House Publishing *Interlochen/Michigan*

How to Declutter with Archangel Jophiel

How to relieve stress, anxiety, and clutter from your life

Z.Z. Rae

Other Books by Z.Z. Rae

- Your Voice Your Choice: The Value of Every Woman
- Ties of the Heart: How to recover from Divorce and Breakups (A 12 step-by-step healing process)
- I Want to be a Unicorn (Why Unicorns are Real and You can be One

Angel Guidance Series

- Angel Guidance for Wealth (Abundant Living for Everyone)
- Angel Guidance for Dreams (Your Dreams Explained by the Angels)
- Angel Guidance for Inner Healing (Heal your Heart, Soul, and Mind with the Angels)
- Angel Guidance for Creativity (Unlock Your Gift)
- Angel Guidance for Peace (Allow life's burdens to fade)
- Angel Guidance for Joy (Raise your Vibrations)
- Angel Guidance for Energy Healing (Aligning your beliefs with your desires)
- Angel Guidance for Awakening Spiritual Gifts (Uncover your natural ability)

Spiritual Tools

- How to Work with Archangels: (Guidance from archangels for abundance, healing, spiritual wisdom, and more.)

Magical Mermaid Messages

- Magical Mermaid Messages on Abundance (How to manifest money with the law of abundance)
- How to Manifest a Soulmate (with a little help from the mermaids)
- How to Manifest a Soulmate Journal (A journal to attract your soulmate)

Books by Natasha House

Grace Alive Series

Christian Romance

- Grace Alive
- Grace Unbroken

Rebirth of the Prophesy Series

Sci-fi Romance

- Fatal Alien Affection
- Fatal Alien Attraction

The Jade Series

Epic Fantasy

- The Vullens' Curse
- The Deities' Touch
- The Vision Stone

Superhero Princess Series

Middle grade/Young Adult

- Zara

Nonfiction

- How to KEEP Writing Your Book
- Illustrated Sermons for Youth or Adults
- Grace Speaks

For my spiritual friends

Intro from Z.Z. Rae

I've never been super organized, so I found it quite funny how Archangel Jophiel wanted to speak to me about this subject. In the last year or two, I've found that I've been decluttering a lot.

The more I've worked with the archangels, the more I realize how they've helped my life in different ways. Archangel Jophiel is more than just the *declutter* angel. She carries a gentle pink energy that is kind, warm, and loving.

When I do readings or help people, Archangel Jophiel often shows up. I recognize her energy right away. I know it sounds funny to say this, but her energy even *feels* pink.

She's always kindly smiling, and like a gentle mother, brings healing, love, and affection to anyone who wants her help.

Decluttering is more than simply donating belongings or throwing things away. It's deeper than that, and you'll grasp that as you read Archangel

Jophiel's messages. I am going to call on her a bunch to help me keep decluttering my mind and life.

Enjoy her messages.

-Z.Z. Rae

Note from the Author

I write what I hear from the divine. Whether it comes from angels, fairies, mermaids, or a divine source. I let their words be authentic. As you dive into this book, have an open mind for the archangels to teach you. Every book I write changes me, and I hope it can bring you healing.

We never worship angels or pray to them, but we can receive help if we are open to it. I believe these angels want to help spread a message of love to everyone who is willing to open their hearts.

-Z.Z. Rae

Chapter 1: Who is Archangel Jophiel?

Insert from my book: How to Work with Archangels

Archangel Jophiel's name means:

Beauty of God

Archangel Jophiel, (sometimes written as Iophiel or Zaphiel) shows up as one of the seven archangels in Pseudo-Dionysius's De Coelesti Hierarchia ("Celestial Hierarchy"). This is a 5th-century text on angelology which has been significant in Christian theology. She is recognized as the angel of illumination and creative power.

It's known that this theology impacted Thomas Aquinas's writings as he talked about the nine choirs of angels. Jophiel sometimes makes an appearance as being extremely tall (over 9 feet), wearing a yellow cloak, and wielding a flaming sword.

In Jewish tradition, Archangel Jophiel was the first mentioned angel. She was the one who drove Adam and Eve out of the Garden of Eden with her flaming sword. Because she had the honor of doing so, she is left to guard the Tree of Life.

Archangel Jophiel's Gifts

Since Archangel Jophiel means, "beauty of God" she has a feminine energy that uplifts situations and brings the beauty out of them. Here are some things she beautifies.

Loving Feelings

If you ask her, Jophiel will flood your heart and body with good feelings of love and gratitude. If you feel a gentle touch on your brow and a loving embrace, that's Jophiel reminding you of all the good in your life.

Home and Office

Decluttering your work space can help uplift your thoughts and energy, so that you can relax. If you feel a nudge to declutter, that could be Jophiel trying to help beautify your environment.

Beautifying Thoughts

When facing negative thoughts, Archangel Jophiel can help you see the beauty in your relationships, life, and the situations you face. She will breathe beauty over your mind to help uplift you each day.

Self-love

If you struggle in the department of self-love or self-care, call on Jophiel to help you beautify your mindset toward yourself. She can help you with feeling better about your appearance and who you are.

Learning New Things

Jophiel loves to lend a helping hand when you are tackling a new thing. When it comes to spiritual matters, she loves to help show you your own potential.

Inspiration

If you're having trouble with inspiration, call on Jophiel to help untangle your thought process. She'll reveal to you your untapped potential you have inside.

Environment

Environmental issues are something Jophiel is passionate about. If you wish to help in that area, call on Jophiel to assist you.

Negative to Positive

Struggling with negative thoughts can be difficult. Call on Archangel Jophiel if you need help transforming your thoughts from negative to positive.

If you are having a hard time in a relationship, you can call on her to help clear up the misunderstanding.

Beauty

Jophiel helps in a lot of areas including assistance with your appearance such as: wardrobe, makeup, and hair.

Helps Clean Out the Old

When you get a sudden urge to start donating or selling items that you no longer need, it's more and likely Archangel Jophiel. She understands how our environment can impact us, so she may start nudging you to clean up the area around you.

Color:

Dark Pink

Crystals or Gemstones:

Rubellite, Deep Pink Tourmaline, Ametrine, Smokey Quartz, and Rutilated Quartz

Scents:

Lavender, Orange, Myrrh, and Lemongrass

Zodiac Sign:

Libra

Archangel Jophiel in a Nutshell

- Loving Feelings
- Home and Office
- Beautifying Thoughts
- Self-love
- Learning New Things
- Inspiration
- Environment
- Negative to Positive
- Beauty
- Helps Clean Out the Old

Message from Archangel Jophiel

Let go of that which no longer serves you. You don't need things that are heavy that drag you down. If you look around your environment and see items that no longer serve you, purge those things, and lovingly let them go. There are times when possessions serve you, and then later on they no longer have a loving purpose for you.

When those items no longer add to your life, it's time to release and surrender those things. The energy of your environment is impacted by those items you hold onto—whether you think they do or not.

Things can impact your energy or mood on a daily basis. If you struggle with your thoughts of a negative nature, simply turn toward the things that please you.

What subjects are uplifting? What makes you feel good? Do you feel good when you look at a picture on your wall? Do you feel good when you look at your child? Think on those things—instead what holds you down. Uplift your energy, darlings.

Affirmation to Archangel Jophiel

"Dear Archangel Jophiel, thank you for helping me purge out what I no longer need in my life. I ask for help to keep my thoughts healthy and happy."

Chapter 2: Setting the Stage

Hello, and good morning (or whatever time you prefer). I'm here to assist you on a few matters today. Organization is a thing many people say I am good at. (Laughs). I suppose I am, but it is really a matter of beautifying what is already there.

When something is cluttered or messy, it isn't that those things are naughty or bad. It is a matter of placing them in a way that makes sense to you and them both.

What you see around you is a matter or reflection of the mind. These items in your home may give you a sense of security, familiarity, or reflection of something you are dealing with.

When things get cluttered, that's where I step into the picture. Many people hold things in their mind that are unneeded.

I might need that sweater one day...

While they reach for the one they love.

I might need that extra pair of mittens...

While they continue to wear what fits them best.

See where I am taking this?

There is something in the mind that causes the clutter to build. It can be hard for people to let go of familiar things…even if it no longer serves them. In many ways, letting go of clutter, is letting go of the past.

If it doesn't serve you, why are you holding onto it?

It's a sense of familiarity that keeps it held in place. The past may serve as many different things. Some situations hurt you, some helped you, or perhaps some memories felt better.

When you hold onto a memory, you regret doing, are you not punishing yourself for that moment in time? This is how many things gain momentum. There are things you regret purchasing which now hold no significance for you. You may feel despondent that you wasted time, money, or energy on those products, so you keep them.

You may have felt tricked into buying it.

Here is where I step in. I am not only going to help you declutter your house, but your mind. For the mind is where the true clutter collects. The manifestation is a symptom of the real thing. The mind holds the key to releasing anything that no longer serves you. Are you ready to dive into our lessons today? Good!

Affirmation

I am ready to declutter my life. I step into a new mindset today.

Chapter 3: Keeping it Real

Let's dig right into this, because I want to help you free yourself from the mindsets that hold the clutter into place. Clutter never feels very good, yet many people keep it around.

Why?

When you purchase something, or you look at something you own, you hold an attachment to it. It cost you something. You put your personal energy into the item you now hold in your hand. So, in order to release it, you must take back the energy from the clutter you hold.

How do I do that?

I'm so glad you asked! As you probably know, everything around you holds vibration or energy. What you may not see is that the item, you hold, is an extension of your thoughts, feelings, and choices. What you chose to think, showed up in your hand one day.

The clutter around you is a result of the thoughts you've invested time into. What do you see around you most?

Is it:

- toys
- books
- clothes
- knickknacks or collectables
- electronics
- unneeded kitchen things
- unused products

What objects hold your attention the most? This is what we will look at today. Let's start off with the basics. No need to tackle too much just yet.

Many people, who want to declutter, will start off with high expectations. They will have confidence that they can get rid of everything they no longer need. Here's what I find quite amusing, yet I still have compassion for…you get rid of it, yet you still hold it.

What Does That Mean?

For example: have you ever gotten rid of clothes, only to find two weeks later your closet cluttered again? Have you dug back into that same closet, only to get rid of more clothes?

Why is that?

You would think that the first time through you'd get rid of everything you no longer wanted or needed.

But did you?

Until you deal with the energy, behind the cluttered closet, it will always remain that—cluttered. I'm sure you've heard of the law of attraction. What does that law implement in your life? Like attracts like, correct? So, if you get rid of the clutter, yet the thoughts of clutter remain, you will only attract more and more clutter into your closet. I use clothes as an example, because clothes can be the culprit for most cluttered houses.

The Feelings Behind the Clutter

Everything you do is with emotion. Not one choice you make is devoid of it, even if it seems that way. You purchase things for a reason. They make you feel better in the moment. You place an attachment on the item you purchased, so it now holds a piece of your energy. This is what I want to discuss with you. The power of that emotion or energy, in the thing, is what holds it in place. When you let go of the energy or emotion, it can return to you, and you can release that item from your life.

Much like an old romance, the item hangs onto your thoughts, because you haven't let it be a lesson that served you in some way.

You've never wasted money on something, because that item can teach you what you need to know. That item can teach you that you don't need it in order to feel better.

You Can Feel Better Right Now

In order to release the old clutter, you must turn inward. Let go of the regret of spending time, energy, or money on that possession. Much like you'd forgive yourself or someone else for a past relationship.

Let it be a lesson learned.

Affirmation

I take back the energy I invested into the items I bought. I release them.

Chapter 4: The Past Reflection

At one point, the things you purchased may have aided your life. That cellphone you bought worked wonders for you for a while, so why do you still keep the old device?

I'm sure you have sweaters or clothes you wore four years ago and paid top dollar for. Did they serve their purpose in their time, and now you've moved into a new style? Do you regret purchasing those items at full price?

Ask yourself a few questions:

- Did this item serve me in its time?
- Do I feel regret about purchasing it?
- Do I feel bad that someone else bought it?

Let's address a few of those questions today.

Did This Item Serve Me in its Time?

Take an item in your hand that you feel no longer serves you. Whatever it is, take a good look at it. Is it outdated? Ask yourself a few questions as to why you kept it.

- Do I feel bad how much it cost?
- Did it serve me in its time?
- Why do I want it still?
- Can I thank it for its service and release it?
- Did I learn a lesson from this item?

Whatever the reasons are for keeping it, it's okay. Don't beat yourself up for the attachments you carry toward the thing you hold.

After you've looked at this belonging, it's time to receive the energy back from it, and let it go. Once you acknowledge that it served you at one point (whether you used it or not) in your mind's eye, see the energy coming back to you. Let go of any and all regret about *wasting money* on this product, because it still gave you a lesson to ponder upon.

Do I Regret Purchasing This?

This can be the biggest issue when it comes to letting an old item go. So many times, people purchase what they don't need. You may have bought it for several reasons:

- A trend
- An emotional purchase (such as pity for the vendor, or to make you feel better)
- Caught up in something new
- Going with the flow
- Thought you needed it
- Liked how it made you feel

Whatever the reason was, it served its purpose for you to reflect on. Maybe you simply liked the thing, and so you acted on that impulse and bought it. Sometimes people purchase something out of nostalgia.

When you're children you play with things that make you feel wonderful, and you attach that feeling of joy to those items. This is why collectors see an item and purchase them, because it fills them with the same sense of wonder as when they were children.

There is nothing wrong with this, but here is where extreme clutter can manifest. The items they hold, are tiny reflections of something much deeper.

If you purchase things out of lack—such as you want to fill an emotional need—it will soon follow with a sense of regret, so that it's hard to release the item.

Wasted money (or energy) can be difficult to deal with on an emotional scale, so as a result, people keep what they don't need anymore. I want to help you by saying: *it's okay that you bought that item, but let it teach you what you need to know, and let it go.*

If you hold regret about wasted money, you will hang onto things that don't feel joyful in your life. Be aware that even stuff can impact your home. If it holds feelings of regret, lack, or negativity, it can clutter your home with that emotion.

Walk yourself through the steps of asking:

- Did this teach me something?
- Can I forgive myself for buying something I didn't need?
- Can I receive the lesson from this purchase and move on?

If you let a purchase teach you a lesson, it was never a waste. If there was no lesson, then you will hold regret over the item.

I know I said it once, but past relationships can hold many, many regrets, and if you do not let the lesson shine through, you will hold the reflection of regret in your current relationships too. Old regrets will clutter your current life. It's much like how old things in your closet clutter your life too.

Once you learn the lesson, it frees you to move past it all.

Affirmation

I choose to learn the lesson in my clutter. I let go of all regrets and forgive myself.

Chapter 5: Someone Else Bought it

This is a big issue with many people. It's not your energy—it's someone else's.

How can I get rid of something someone spent money, energy, and invested love into?

I know this is a big one, and it's hard for countless individuals. Especially if that loved one has passed—the energy in the item is intensified. Not that I'm saying get rid of things that are meaningful to you from a loved one, but here's a few questions for you to ask yourself.

- Do I use this item someone bought me?
- Do I want this?
- Do I feel bad I don't use what they bought?
- Do I feel negative when I look at this?

If you have a hard time getting rid of clutter that someone else bought, here's a fresh outlook on it. When they bought it for you, they projected a part of their energy into it. They may have thought it was for you, but have you ever gotten stuff from someone that they liked, not you? It's as if they bought it for themselves.

I'm sure you know countless folks who tend to purchase this way. Some people buy with you in mind, so it seems a bit more accurate. Either way, I know it is a challenge to get rid of it. Here's a few things you can reflect on to release it.

- Did I feel happy they thought of me?
- Can I give it to someone who will love it?
- Can I release it with love?

If you receive the joy from the giving of the item; even if you didn't like it, then it becomes much easier to let it go. It served its purpose. If someone you know will enjoy the item more, there is no harm in releasing it to them.

Joy Can Be Shared

When you receive an item from someone it is an act of love. Giving shares joy between two people. If you view the item as a shared joy, it is much easier to release it with a spirit of love behind it. That item will be appreciated by someone else in a different way.

Share the love by gifting, donating, or reusing it in some way that spreads more joy with another.

Affirmation

I let go of gifts from others. It's okay to share that joy with someone else.

Chapter 6: Cleansing the Room

You've probably heard of many ways to cleanse a home. I want to bring a fresh outlook on this subject matter. When you walk into a room, how does it feel? Does it feel fresh, happy, or joyful? This is what we will look at today in this chapter.

A home is a place of peace, or this is the way it should be. If things around you feel scattered, cluttered, or full of low-energy, you must release those items. This can simply be moving things around to freshen the look of the home, removing old items which no longer serve you, or putting a fresh coat of paint on something.

Plants

Putting alive plants in a home can bring a sense of calm. I often instruct others to purchase things that bring an *aliveness* to the home, and plants are the perfect ingredient for that. If you have to choose between an old knickknack, or a plant, choose to keep the plant. It will add a sense of joy in your environment.

Prayer Scrubbing

Lifting old furniture, with a bit of paint, can brighten an atmosphere in an instant. Sometimes a piece of furniture or an item needs a good prayer scrubbing.

I know some of you may think this is strange, but have you heard of items bringing people bad vibes? This is because the item soaked in the negative thoughts of its inhabitants for a long time, so it took on the energy as its own. This is not to frighten you, but if you do sense something from a piece of furniture you purchased, simply say a little prayer over it, and you should be as right as rain.

Music

Play music in your home to brighten the atmosphere. Lifting the furniture, utensils, and items with joyful tunes, will help them assist you better. When you bless those things in your home, they will be filled with joyfulness in their very essence.

If you haven't heard of these types of things, I advise you to study some of the tests about plants or water. Physical things absorb thoughts, and it can bring a low vibration or a high vibration to your atmosphere.

Us angels believe in the livingness of everything. Everything you see, hear, touch, and smell has a living essence to it. You may not see it, but it is all vibrating at different levels. When you get a sense to move something around, discard it, or give it away—follow that impulse. Especially if you are feeling the need to declutter or clear out some old energy in your soul.

You'll find discarding things makes your mind, heart, and body feel lighter and lighter. This is because you are changing the energy of your home by ridding yourself of old clutter.

Affirmation

I follow my instinct to lighten the atmosphere of my home.

Chapter 7: The Power of Decluttering

There is a sense of power when you discard things you don't need. You pull back the energy you spread into those items, so that you feel happier, lighter, and overall more at ease. This is because the energy, which was stored in those unneeded items, returned to you. If you understand the reason why you held onto those objects, you can make the slight changes internally, so that you don't return to purchasing another thing you don't need.

I want to help you stay feeling empowered in your life. If you see flashes of pink or green, that would be me. If you are drawn to pink or green, that is also me.

I know we are addressing a lot about the home, but I also want to talk about decluttering the mind.

There are many rooms in the mind. Some things that you dwell on are old clutter. The more you address the old clutter, the lighter and happier you will feel. It will start to reflect on the outside as well—cleaner home—less old energy. They are tightly interwoven.

You cannot declutter your home, without decluttering your mind. Like I spoke about, if the root issue is still there, it will only attract more of the same—as the law of attraction states.

When you release the energy that was stored in the mind, you release energy that is stored in the physical plane. This is why when you go to declutter, you may feel a range of different emotions. When you pick something up, how does it make you feel?

- Joy
- Guilt
- Lack
- Anxiety
- Peace
- Love
- Responsibility
- Regret
- Usefulness
- Ease

If it brings a negative emotion, ask yourself why. Why do you feel regret, fear, anxiety, or guilt about that item? Choose to see the lesson, and offer love instead. Once you do, you can release it.

This isn't always easy for people, and I understand that completely. I see how old objects hold value—but sometimes the value is a negative feeling. Perhaps you are feeling guilty that you want to get rid of an old item from your mother's. It's time to release the guilt, learn the lesson, and move past it.

Here is where I gently take your hand and beautify your thoughts. Your mother, whether passed away or alive, wants you to be happy. If the item only brings a sense of regret, guilt, rejection, or fear, she'd want you to release it. Even if your mother wasn't the best parent, her true self is full of love for you, and she would desire that.

Let's try something together. Pick up something that someone gave you. Look at it carefully. Acknowledge the emotion it brings you. If it brings a sense of joy, yet you still don't want it, let it fill you with joy for a moment longer. Once it does, set it in a pile to donate.

Pick up each thing you no longer feel is needed, and let the joy of that item give you one last goodbye. If there never was joy in the item, see the lesson in the midst of it. Grasp why you kept it, even though it did not bring you joy.

Grow From the Experience, and Release It

Whatever the emotion you sense from something around you, tune into it, and then uncover what you want to do from that point. Many times, when something makes one of you uncomfortable, you simply hide it away. Except, the energy of it is still in your home. You will still sense it under the surface.

I'm not asking you to tackle everything at once, but if you can declutter items that hold old energy, you'll find yourself feeling freer and freer each day. There are many tips to declutter, and I advise you to research some if you need more help.

This little guide is to help jump start you forward on the journey of decluttering your heart, soul, mind, and body. It starts inward, and it brings an outward expression.

Do you have days when you want to clean up everything? This can be what I lovingly call a 'reset' day. The mind wants to get rid of old stuff that bogs it down, so it creates an impulse in you to get rid of clutter.

Follow this impulse, and let it bring you to a brand-new energy. You'll find the decluttering gives you a fresh perspective on what you love.

Affirmation

I empower myself with a fresh energy.

Chapter 8: Brighten Up

Let's look at old things that need a fresh look. Do you have some old furniture you love, yet it seems a bit old fashioned or drab? Here's a few tips to help brighten up the look. If you don't have much time or energy for a big project, here's a couple things to help.

- A pretty cloth covering

If you don't have a ton of time to paint that end table or dresser, perhaps a pretty cloth will help spruce it up.

- Hire someone

If you have a bit of extra cash, why not hire your teenager or someone else to paint it for you? Better yet, if you know a local artist, perhaps they'd take it on as a portfolio project.

- Move it

At times it's not the piece of furniture itself, but rather where it's located. If the colors are clashing in one room, why not bring it to a different room, and see how it feels to rearrange the area.

This can change up the energy of the home. You'll be able to get a fresh perspective if you want that piece of furniture or not.

- Sell it

There are always people who are looking for an inexpensive piece of furniture. You can advertise it as a great project to refurnish. There are lots of crafty people out there.

Purchase Organizers

Sometimes you buy an organizer to hide more clutter, but this is for you who truly need the items in which you are organizing. If you have shoes, with no home, perhaps purchasing cute bins would keep the cluttered look down.

Old Projects

You'll get to that broken thing, right? I know that's the hard part about decluttering. You run into old projects, which you swore you'd do months ago, and still you put them off. These are the projects that you can lovingly learn a lesson from and move past.

Even if that project cost you something, you can receive the joy of what it first gave you.

Did you feel crafty, accomplished, or happy when you thought about doing that project? Good. Ask yourself how you feel about it now. Does it make you feel dread to complete it?

If so, get rid of the project altogether. That will only bring the energy of your mind into a bundled mess. Old projects had good intentions, and it's okay if they never got completed. It doesn't make you a bad person just because you bought a DIY necklace, only to buy a brand new one at the store.

It may have felt fun at the time to put something like that together. Feel the joy one last time and lovingly let that DIY project go to someone else. Maybe it will make them feel that same excitement you felt for a time.

Creative Ventures

Everyone gets those fun, sparking ideas of creativity. You want to start your own Etsy store, create a book, paint something, or a host of other creative things. Perhaps you bought a book on finances, a program to help you learn Spanish, or something of that sort.

When you look at that creative venture, how does it feel? Do you feel emotions of negativity, or is there a sense of accomplishment in what you did do?

Again, find the lesson in the unfinished creative project.

Affirmation

I find the lesson in what I have, and I let go of what I don't need.

Chapter 9: The Simpler the Better

It's much easier to start a project off in a simplistic way. When something seems HUGE to tackle, it is a natural instinct to avoid that project. When you think about decluttering your home, what does it feel like?

The first step is to identify how you feel about decluttering.

Once you recognize the emotion, break it down into tiny steps to deal with it.

- **Do you feel you need help with this project?**
- **Can you ask for help from someone—if only to support your endeavor?**
- **What is drawing your attention first?**

List of Items

- Clothing
- Books
- Knickknacks or collectables
- Papers

- Sentimental things
- Files (electronic)
- Toys
- Jewelry
- Electronics
- DIY Projects
- Unfinished Projects

There are different ways to take on each one of these things. The best approach is to simplify it. There are many different teachers of organization, but all of you have a personal preference. This personal approach is how you should take on the project of decluttering.

If you have three hours to work on decluttering, start where you feel you can accomplish something. If that is clothing—start there. If it's books—start there. Let yourself know you've accomplished something good, even if there is more organizing to do.

It Starts Off in the Mind

The more you simplify it to your mind, the more the mind will work with you to declutter what it needs.

What about that particular item draws you to declutter? Do you feel your clothing is bogging you down? Start there. Pick up each piece, and ask yourself some questions.

- Have I worn this in the last 6 months?
- What do I feel about this piece of clothing?
- Can I let go of regret of purchasing something I didn't wear?
- Am I only keeping this because someone else bought it or gave it to me?

If you can identify the energy behind why you're keeping something—you'll be able to go through the declutter process much quicker.

Old Identities

Often people purchase something, because they are in a trend. For example: Z.Z. used to love *Darth Vader, Doctor Who, and Batman.* Over a period of time, she received clothing, collectables, mugs, and even bought a framed picture.

Those things were her identity for a bit. She enjoyed them in their time, but now she's shifted onto new things. As a child, she loved fairies, unicorns, and mermaids. Now, her attention is back on those things.

When you feel guilty getting rid of something from an old identity, it's time to let that go. You were once someone who enjoyed those types of things, but you've grown past it now. That's okay. If you've invested a lot of money, time, and energy into collecting certain possessions, can you thank those things for making you feel good in their season?

Children go through stages like this all the time. They will be drawn to certain toys, books, or movies. Once they move past it, they don't want those old things anymore. As a parent, you understand that, and you allow your child to grow past their old identities.

Allow yourself the same privilege. The things you've collected reflect an identity. People bought you stuff, in the past, because it was an act of love. Pick up the old things and lovingly thank them for giving you joy in their time. Then let them go. Donate, sell, or give them away to someone who enjoys them.

Affirmation

I let go of old identities. I move forward.

Chapter 10: Declutter Crash Course

Now that you have a little clearer understanding of why decluttering is important, I want to teach you a few simple steps to get you going. I know we've talked a lot about it, but I want to sum it up for you.

Let's start with something most people have a lot of—clothing.

Project 1

Clothing

Empty your drawers of everything, and lay them down on your bed. Put on music that's soothing for your mind, and grab the first piece of clothing.

- Identify why you have it
- Ask yourself if it served its purpose
- Put it in a "keep" or "donate" pile

After you've decided what to do with each piece of clothing, stand firm in that decision. Sometimes people will revert back and grab out the clothing they just discarded. If you still feel an attachment, you may have to go through the letting go process again.

Here's some common thoughts to why:

I spent a lot on it.

I never wore it, and I feel bad.

I used to like it.

I might wear it one day.

I might wear it to be fancy.

What if I need it, and I got rid of it?

Someone gave it to me.

If any of these thoughts pop into your head, explore them a bit. Do you feel you won't have what you need, when you need it? Are you associating that item with guilt or regret?

Bargain Guilt

You may have purchased an item at a low cost, and now feel bad you spent any money at all, because you never truly wanted it to begin with. The mind may add up all the money you've spent on clothing that ended up being donated.

Sometimes you purchase things out of impulse because of the low cost. Here's a trick I like to help people with. When you see that low-cost piece of clothing ask yourself:

How do I feel when I hold this?

Do I feel poor?

Do I feel nice?

Will I wear this a lot?

If you purchased that item out of a lack mentality—it will only hold that energy. If you purchased it, because you truly loved it, it served its purpose. Clothing absorbs many things. Whatever you've put into something, it will reflect back.

Project 2

Books

Do you have piles of books that are unread? This is a pretty common thing. If you enjoy reading, you may have purchased a book for a variety of reasons.

- A trend

- Low-cost
- Looked interesting
- Study
- A friend recommended it

I try to help people with this, because I know it can be hard to get rid of things you invested energy into. Books hold the author's energy all the way through it. If you picked up this book, you were drawn to the energy of it—not just the subject.

Every person has their stamp of energy on their words. You may have bought a strewn of books at one point, only to realize later you didn't have time or interest anymore in that genre or subject matter.

A book can release a vibe in your home, so you may have been drawn to the high-vibration of the book itself. It's time to ask yourself some questions.

- How do I feel when I touch this book?
- Did it serve its purpose in its time?
- Will I read this in the next year?
- Can I lovingly let it go?
- Why am I keeping this book?

- Do I like the energy this book brings me?

As you pick up each book, explore these questions, until you know the answer. Once you know why you're hanging onto something, you have the power to let it go or keep it.

Create two piles.

- Keep
- Donate

When you keep it, create a loose plan of reading it in the next year or at the latest two years. Once you've read a book, ask yourself: *do I need to keep this now?*

Project 3

Knickknacks and Collectables/Misc.

Everyone likes something. There are collectors all over the world, and unless you've mastered living in a very simplistic way, I'm sure you have some sort of knickknacks or collectables in your home. When you go through these, it's a bit different. You may have spent money over the years—maybe thousands on your collection. Here's how to tackle this project.

Ask yourself:

- Is this an old identity?
- Do I feel guilty how much I've spent on these?
- Do I like this?
- How does this make me feel now?
- Am I keeping this because of someone else?

Once you understand why you have your collectables or knickknacks, you can make a choice to release them or keep them.

When you declutter a room, you'll find old things that are expired, or things you may shove aside for now. Look at those things one by one, and allow yourself the freedom to discard them one at a time.

Project 4

Papers

Paper likes to collect everywhere. You may find that it's a challenge to keep it to a minimum. Old bills, letters, cards, or receipts may pile up around you. Create a habit of recycling papers right after you get them. Once you find yourself in that flow, you'll find the clutter going down in a dramatic way.

Project 5

Sentimental

This can be the hardest for people to tackle, because not only does it hold *more* energy, it can hold a variety of memories attached to it. You may have collected old letters, cards, children's projects, or toys from the past. Go through each item, *slowly*, because this can be more of an emotional experience than the other projects. Ask yourself:

- How do I feel about this?
- Do I find joy in remembering this?
- Can I let this go now?

Once you identify how you feel, create a beautiful safe space for your memories to rest. If you'd like to create a memory journal, scrapbook, or display, it can help sort out what memories you'd like to hold onto.

Affirmation

I can easily declutter my home.

Chapter 11: Go With the Flow

Go with the flow. It's much easier to do anything when you feel at ease with yourself about it. If you tackle a decluttering project with a lot of dread, you won't be able to clear away what you need. It will be more of a challenge to release joy into your atmosphere. If a project feels bogged down, wait until you have the right spark to go with it.

Whenever you need a boost of peaceful energy, call on me, and I will help you tackle those much-needed decluttering projects. Remember, it can take time to really cleanse a home of old energy. You're not superman, so don't expect to get it all done in one day. The more confidence you build in yourself, you'll see the result in how you take care of your living space.

Remember a few tips.

You Attract What You Think

If you think you are cluttered and disorganized, it will show up in your life again and again. If you feel you are making strides to organize, it will show up in your energy as a physical result. Working on any project is an outcome of what you're putting into it. When it comes to decluttering, it's okay if you have your own pace. The more you clear the low-vibration out of your personal energy, the more you'll see it show up in your living environment.

Get into the natural rhythm of your energy. Once you understand that your natural state is ease, you'll see it showing up more and more in your home. Creating new habits can take a bit of time, but I want to encourage you to keep going!

Affirmation

I go with the flow. I am at ease with myself.

Chapter 12: List

Here's a list to make these projects easier.

In the Kitchen

- Extra cups and mugs (how many can your household realistically use?)
- Plastic cutlery
- Unused plastic containers, especially if they don't have a lid
- Travel mugs that are ugly/missing lids/don't keep things hot or cold well
- Expired food
- Cookie cutters you don't use
- Multiple pairs of scissors (keep only two if you must keep multiple)
- Duplicate kitchen utensils
- Cake pans you don't use
- Extra mason jars

In the Bathroom

- Outdated drugs or vitamins
- Excess bobby pins
- Unused perfume or colognes
- Makeup you've never used
- Makeup that has expired
- Dried up nail polishes
- Half used lip balm containers
- Expired sunscreen
- Curling irons or straighteners you don't use
- Extra travel size shampoo bottles

In the Bedrooms

- Socks with holes or without mates
- Jewelry you don't wear
- Clothes that are more than 2 sizes too big or small
- Clothing that you haven't worn in the last 6 months to a year

- Old sneakers
- Extra plastic hangers
- Purses you don't use

Paper Clutter

- Old bills
- Old newspapers
- Ticket stubs
- Paychecks older than 2 years
- Old day planners
- Extra notebooks
- Old calendars
- Boxes
- Old Christmas cards
- Expired coupons
- Take out menus (you can easily find this information online)

Linens & Decor

- Rugs or decor you don't use

- Extra bed linens (you should have two sets per bed)
- Extra cleaning rags
- Extra pillows
- Knick knacks you don't like or don't display
- Candles you don't use
- Tea light candles (use them or lose them)

Technology & Entertainment

- Magazines (you can read hundreds of them online, some of them for free)
- Old technology such as CDs, VHS tapes (especially if you don't own a player), etc.
- Movies you won't watch again
- Toys that never get played with
- Books you will never read again
- More ear buds than you have family members
- Games with missing pieces
- Videogames or board games you never play
- Cords that don't belong to anything you currently own

- Travel alarm clock (use your phone)
- Duplicate power cords that never get used
- Old phone covers or screen protectors
- Stuffed animals your kids don't love anymore

Everything Else

- Projects that are half-finished
- Old product boxes
- Matches you'll never use
- Loose screws, nuts, bolts, etc.
- Old paint
- Old party supplies
- Old wedding favors
- Things you bought and still haven't returned (take them back!)
- Cleaning supplies you don't use
- Flower pots (either plant a flower or toss the pot)
- Watering cans, if you don't have plants or flowers, or if you have more than one

- Holiday decor you don't use
- Extra buttons
- Extra highlighters
- Samples of any kind that you aren't using
- Miscellaneous ribbons or string
- Organizers that aren't in use
- Keychains you don't use
- Tape measures (keep one and donate the rest)
- Old craft supplies

I hope this helped you feel empowered to declutter your life. If you ever need encouragement, call on me to help you organize. I love giving my gentle energy as you sort through things that you no longer need in your living space.

Affirmation

I have the power to declutter my life.

Thank you for reading:

How to Declutter with Archangel Jophiel

Visit: eepurl.com/cV-Trf for your

FREE

GIFT

Angel Guidance for Wealth

If you've enjoyed this book, I would love for you to post a review. As an author, I am always learning and growing, and I'd love to hear back from you.

Come visit me on:

Facebook: Z.Z.'s Angel Card Corner

Instagram: @Z.Z.Rae

Blog: www.angelguidancetoday.wordpress.com

Facebook Group: Angel Guidance, Fairies, Mermaids, and Unicorns Magical Realm

Website: https://authorzzrae.wixsite.com/zzrae

YouTube: ZZ Rae ASMR

Other Books by Z.Z. Rae

- Your Voice Your Choice: The Value of Every Woman
- Ties of the Heart: How to recover from Divorce and Breakups (A 12 step-by-step healing process)
- I Want to be a Unicorn (Why Unicorns are Real and You can be One

Angel Guidance Series

- Angel Guidance for Wealth (Abundant Living for Everyone)
- Angel Guidance for Dreams (Your Dreams Explained by the Angels)
- Angel Guidance for Inner Healing (Heal your Heart, Soul, and Mind with the Angels)
- Angel Guidance for Creativity (Unlock Your Gift)
- Angel Guidance for Peace (Allow life's burdens to fade)
- Angel Guidance for Joy (Raise your Vibrations)
- Angel Guidance for Energy Healing (Aligning your beliefs with your desires)
- Angel Guidance for Awakening Spiritual Gifts (Uncover your natural ability)

Spiritual Tools

- How to Work with Archangels: (Guidance from archangels for abundance, healing, spiritual wisdom, and more.)

Magical Mermaid Messages

- Magical Mermaid Messages on Abundance (How to manifest money with the law of abundance)
- How to Manifest a Soulmate (with a little help from the mermaids)
- How to Manifest a Soulmate Journal (A journal to attract your soulmate)

Books by Natasha House

Grace Alive Series

Christian Romance

- Grace Alive
- Grace Unbroken

Rebirth of the Prophesy Series

Sci-fi Romance

- Fatal Alien Affection
- Fatal Alien Attraction

The Jade Series

Epic Fantasy

- The Vullens' Curse
- The Deities' Touch
- The Vision Stone

Superhero Princess Series

Middle grade/Young Adult

- Zara

Nonfiction

- How to KEEP Writing Your Book
- Illustrated Sermons for Youth or Adults
- Grace Speaks

Printed in Great Britain
by Amazon